MOOR MUSIC

for Andrew Bartz and the music

Mike Jenkins
MOOR MUSIC

SEREN

Seren is the book imprint of
Poetry Wales Press Ltd.
57 Nolton Street, Bridgend, Wales, CF31 3AE
www.serenbooks.com

The right of Mike Jenkins to be identified as
the author of this work has been asserted in accordance
with the Copyright, Designs and Patents Act, 1988.

© Mike Jenkins 2010.

ISBN: 978-1-85411-535-5

A CIP record for this title is available from the British Library.

All rights reserved. No part of this publication may be reproduced,
stored in a retrieval system, or transmitted at any time or by any means,
electronic, mechanical, photocopying, recording or otherwise without
the prior permission of the copyright holder.

The publisher acknowledges the financial assistance of the Welsh Books Council.

Cover paintings by David Tress
Front: 'Finding Winter Gorse', mixed media on paper, 30x40cm.
Back: 'And What I Found Was A Cold Day', mixed media on paper, 40x61cm.

Printed in Bembo by Berforts.

Author's website/blog: www.mikejenkins.net

Contents

Overture: The Awakening	7
Moor Music	8
Bonfire on the Waun	9
Force-fields: Aberdar Mt.	10
December Roses	11
Snow, Another Country	12
Even the Black Cow	13
Came the Ram	14
The Brooding Sleep	15
Park Smile	16
Birds on High Wires	17
Into the Wind	18
Living in Times to Come	19
Like John Clare	20
Sleep-walking on Rust	21
To Sing the Common	22
Gyre-Child	24
The Day of the Bombings	25
Cello Partner	26
Eyes Shut Tight	27
Nightclub Fairies	28
Chipoil Ave.	29
Einstein at the Comp.	30
Encircling	31
A Bonfire in Brittany	32
Kreizenn Ar Son	33
Fado Singer	34
Komitas	35
The Tears of Pablo Neruda	36
Legacies of Pinochet	38
Every Palm a Map	39
Up the Silver Birch	41

Glyndŵr Rd.	42
Dog-hour	43
The Remains	44
Flags of Neon	46
War Stories	47
Dust Anybody?	51
Green-car	52
The Groper	53
The Holes	54
Cycle of Malcontents	55
Clouds Collapse	56
Women of Bryngaer	57
A Shrine	58
Star-searching	59
Passing	61
Oisín's Last Poem	62
The Scallop	63
Diving into the Dark	64
Insomniac Jazz	65
A Once Strange Face	66
The Boy & The Grand	67
A Manic Conductor	68
Gorse Grows Back	69
Acknowledgements	71

Overture : The Awakening

i.m. Jack Gilbert

    4 am through the open window
        louding in -
      Overture: The Awakening

an orchestra of reed-players
  of so many songs
    each mouth an 'O'
       interwoven from grass and moss
      from twigs and even
     discarded litter sprigs

               a year hence
                     he would have run
                down the Taff Trail
              to much-same performance

     his heart percussive
       timpani taut
      and tuned skin

             it stretched so tight
           a single needle pierced it
               instead of muffled heads

  I purposefully place
    a pause in the score
              to re-birth his breathing.

Moor Music

These are instruments you cannot construct

      reeds in winter wind

                          sinewy nerve-lines

hollowed tree

      bass body

           owl bassoon

           down down stream

                        leaf keys

                                  blood crescendoing

the music you cannot notate

     duet of ring doves

                    echo of the snow

        a wind band of starlings
           mimicking the other sections

     and the sigh
     always the sigh

              of the oak's lonely conducting.

Bonfire on the Waun

All day the boys
               have fetched and piled

    with wheelbarrow comically
      bump-lumping across the Waun

    foraged for wood and waste

this Sunday
        Guy Fawkes
               bonfire night

                      they built like termites
                      they carried like ants
                          they busied like squirrels

    (when we say 'No!'
            she cannot comprehend –
    all she wants to see
      are sparkles   colours   explosions –
        squealing close to friends

                how could she know
                those pyres where masks
                were turned into ashes
                blown down the drains
                by fierce, mocking winds
                from so many mouths?)

she window-gazes
      amazes
          as the bonfire rises up
                towards a hanging gunpowder cloud

        wings without body
           disappearing into a hole
        the star-scattering rocket
        has burnt in the sky.

Force-fields: Aberdar Mt.

    Place of no names
                    no tracks remain
where fields unravel their definitions
   without wire or wall

 where paths are laid
by hoof   they whirl
  the overgrown tips

  where rills and rivulets
    are archaeologists
 digging up coal/clinker/flint

   place where boundaries
     are ignored
  or implied by ancient oaks

     which exists out there
       in a fiction

(bound by barbs
 and the larches' strict discipline)

           force-fields
                  go beyond –
      written on by horse-moons
       by comet-trails of birds

  rain rubbing off mud-prints
    feet's fleeting stars.

December Roses

    Black rises

                                astonishingly
                                                  two roses

  a coat of heather shed
    and the old coal
      declares its presence
        of scrabbling screes

                        most leaves have dropped
                        despite frost
                                      two buds
                          red tips
                                      beginning to show

      as though
            nothing would grow again
      as though
            the underground would take revenge

              when fog descends
                to gulp down spoil-heaps

              those roses are two spots
              of blood on a wound
              which could stretch
              from pole to pole

        the currents and the gases –
          the warnings of December roses
the hill-fort of fog
      will be lifted
            bracken and heather
                    ring like an ancient barrow
     petals –
        flaps of skin
            from a cut
                deepening.

Snow, Another Country

Across the moorland
                she leads the way
                              into a new territory
      bootprints spelling her discovery

    no heed
            of ditch or bog –
                          the swan-light
                            the frozen sun
                                    the thistles' antennae

       she runs
            we follow
                      across the Waun
                                wedded
        to this crystal finery

    she takes us back –
    all snowball children
    sleighing whoopery

                      tonight she will dream
                  of the two dwarf snowmen
                  stick arms, eyes of berries –
                      disappearing into the sky

wake to find
        crocuses wilting
                lambs lost in drifting
                          higher than her 4 years

    yet still
          another country
                    has come to visit –
          place before she was born
            when clouds broke
          and blizzards were blown.

Even the Black Cow

Even the cow gets tired
  of the crows on its back
    crows on its back

      picking   flicking   flapping

alive with grubs and fleas

    so they scoot from faraway trees
      as though
          the cow
              had grown
                    wings and claws
                    wings and claws

Even the cow
      no longer standing still
        but following the pastures uphill

      suddenly grows weary
      of the persistent jab
      of ever-hungry birds

        and whips its tail
          jerks back its head

a rawness to the bone
  set her in motion –
    the moist moor grass
      ripped and chewn

                Even the cow
                  black as the crows
                  on its cloud of green,
                    must move on.

Came the Ram

Scrag-end
        dog-eared
                shaggy-coated
                        from a side lane came the ram

      not sheepish
               he ran the main road uphill
                            cars dodging

     twisty-horned
            bull's-eyed
                  unbowed to green
           he hoofed towards
           the bleating bus-stop boys
               who took refuge in a drive

      he veered towards the manicured gardens
          on look-out for the flock

                            a day later in our Close
                            still searching

besmirched
        thick-matted
                dark pricked
    isolated
          yet silent
              hoarse voice within
                        worrying away
   eating at his skin
            some rot, some disease
                     no dip could remedy

       free to roam
            in bounds of body.

The Brooding Sleep
Roath Park Lake

The 'cello-swan-
                feathered bark of Saint-Saens
    not a dying call
    long lost adagio

but
    an inner song
           of glide and flight
                      drawing curtains on reflective light

the brooding sleep
   of both male and female
     on a nest of mud-caked reeds
      among the litter flung
        off-key packets and cans

                an inner song
                of five ovals
                    curiously grey-brown
              below the path, the bridge

        where the white clock
         knows no time

     the 'cello-boat floats
      across the lake
        till signets are born.

Park Smile

    Think of it

           a park
                a woman
                        her smile bisects
                        the exact flower-beds –
                        call her April
                        yet a stranger

two birds zitter above the lake
their mating aerial combat
                        the sun-balloon in celebration
                        of another smile born

              you can see it
              half a mile away
              and coming, coming
(but, she has a black dog –
a smile's never alone)
              you are still mesmerised –
              mouth is tulip opening

                        watch her pass
                        out of sight forever,
                        black dog leading

      think of it

              the lake so murky
              no reflections
  yet, that smile
        makes a face under the surface
          as she swivels her hips
            round the corner, as you'll never
            catch its light again.

Birds on High Wires

Up on the high wires
I heard them first –
a charm of finches

persistent
                Chick,chick,chick!

telephone lines
         the staves –
                   green notes from a distance
a trick of the sun
     through binoculars
            white-capped
                a flash of white
                        across wings
     as though
         premonitions
              of ice and snow

(I'd seen the weather map
   systems from the north
     not south Atlantic warm wet
       but winds with icy breath –

       did they know too
             even if
                today was highest blue?

when they flew
   in feeding fits and starts
     their butterfly motions
      were fragile as the season

before owltime
     they had gone
              it was a resting place
                on a long migration
                   in search of the sun

     the telephone wires silent and bare –
     a manuscript without a song.

Into the Wind

She strode off
  up the Waun
    knowing no barriers
      her mutters cutting

        brown hair blown back
          she wouldn't stop —
        escaping at last
          the walls' shuddering

he'd said — **Let her go!**
  She'll walk it off!
    she yelled — **Come back!**
Don't be so daft!

      they treated her like a kid
        she couldn't go anywhere
          for fear of who she met —
            even town a foreign threat

she knew they'd regret —
  springing on reed beds
    she rushed into the wind
      like a bolting horse

        till she reached the stream
        didn't want to be seen —
        the oaks her camouflage
        a cloak of gorse

till she reached the top
  and her house was a block
    once toyed with
      on the carpet

        and their nags and shouts
          were left tattered on wire —
          she could gaze down on
        another valley   another future.

Living in Times to Come

                                          Every day now
                              more so
            living in times to come

beginning with messages
                  late August oak leaves
                            falling brown
                                      blown-in prophecies

       the rain that turns houses into caravans

           manhole covers sucked up
               landslides toppling trees covering railways
                 roads submerged under a muddy deluge
                   bridges collapsing like brittle branches

           schools becoming islands in a morning –
           as panicky pupils become evacuees
               ordered to march to higher ground

     this weather weirding
                 more sinister

we take the slow bus home
     climbing up to the mountain-tops
          looking down on a chasm of cloud

                  the patterned piles of drystone walls
                  with leaning blocks in lines
                       more resolute than many homes

sandbags gushed aside
   like a tide on dunes
                     upturned umbrellas
                        dead crows on pavingstones

          the future rap-rap-rapping
            at every pane
               to be let in.

Like John Clare

I can hear him
    railing against enclosures
            rights of peasant folk
                    on the Common Land
                stolen by landowners'
                high stone borders

overnight
    across the Waun
        a line of fence-posts
                marks for an operation

     but no face-lift
           (cauterizing of industrial tumour)

    rather
        the pointless gouging of old skin
          (pocked by warts   wrinkles   burst veins)
        the face of Aberdâr mountain

to ready the land for quarrying
            coal the depth of our nightmares

        (they can never weave back
        those intricate nests

     never grow again
        the moor's flowery covering
           of lady's smock and feathery bog-cotton

    like Clare
        my cuckoo-mind
                has become a pugilist

    I would attack the wire
              in the hood of the night.

Sleep-walking on Rust

      the pulling up of carpets
      calling names into the gap

      the standing naked at the window
      staring, oblivious to the scene

above all
      the walking on rust

              (how the wind brings it back –
              whistling of sea-memories
            of childhood sheets
             made into sails
              of coats ballooning
                on the hill's rim)

the walking on leaves
  turned metallic –
oak and birch
  sycamore and horse-chestnut
  become copper and brass

      so the wind
             knocks at every door

    I stray from my bound bed
      to let it enter

but the rust
        grates my soles
             wakes my skin

    I hear the gale outside –
      Let me in! Let me in!

To Sing the Common
i.m. Gilespi

And the flute
          came down
                    from the branch

                              to become a walking-stick
                              for an old man –
                              a pointer for the sun –
                              a twig racing rapidly –
                              a rainbow boomerang

the sax
        once a statue
                  of a snake

                          its tongue
                                      a river-fork –
                      its many skins
                                      cast off
                  as it played
                                a different tune
                  for each incarnation

the viola emerged from hibernation

                  drawn by the sun
                by shoots and buds
              it leapt across fences
                its tail the bow balancing
                  and everything it did
                      was the opposite of sleeping

the cello lost its darkness
                in the open space
                      became a calf
                      taut string limbs
                          exploring every blade –
                      it flexed between
                        low and high land

the lead and bass
                were fallen wires

                              they rooted among rocks
                            once tracks of a drift-mine –
                              the electricity of sap
                              fed the berries
                                              wild and gritty

from out of the shaft
                    the piano was hauled up

                    at first
                              they thought it was a ghost

                    till it sang like a canary released –
                    way-hayed like a pony
                    freed from a gallery

and the drums
              those drams
                         taking
                              no longer coal
                                              but
                                              cloud-cargoes
                    whinberries   wild mint   & strawberries

the voice of water
                    coursing over and under

                              embracing the dragonfly star
                              return of the sunbreasted kingfisher
                              the buzzard's plummeting comet

              under a full-moon spotlight

              this unlikely band
                    gathered

              to sing the Common.

Gyre-Child

    A hurricane   a tornado
    no wind   no storm

                  just energy
                          unbound
  on the dance-floor
    the elements four
      of bass, drum, saxophone, guitar

she becomes
        the jazz
            a whirligig
                  a spinning-top

    peat-brown   she burns inside herself –
  we glow as we're watching

      no need
    of a partner –
  elders spurned

      no set steps
    for an Isadora –
    a windmilling
     whirling turn

      our gyre-child
    all wiry-veined –
      dizzily larking

till the cymbals' last spark.

The Day of the Bombings

It could have been
it could have been you
it could have been you there

if
if you hadn't gone
if you hadn't gone for a coffee

you left the tube
close to that man
close to the wired man

moving
moving towards Westminster
heading for the offices of power

but a student
work another layer
a layer worn like a jacket

it could have been you
blown to blood
burst and scattered

your slim limbs
all your wiriness
spread like waste

all your intelligence
your musical hands
like broken instruments

when signals
when waves reached
when I spoke to you at last

you were walking
you were treading water
among those channels of commuters

I still carry
I still carry that note –
you may know someone, you may want......

Cello Partner

A slim, upright mirror –
  stories of stacked books,
    metronome on the dressing-table

      street-sounds of turning cars in the Close
        scrawl through the open window
          (for air   for breath)

        he tunes up, ear down
          nerves reaching to the tips
            of fingers on each lettered string

              at first there are insects droning
                from his bow and then
                  single notes of warblers, larks

                  he fills the mirror now
                    checks his posture and sets
                      the tick of tempo pacing

              scales and runs up and down –
                his arms and his bow
                  are a couple in fandango

        the double bed made up,
          the unfamiliar titles –
            but room for music to grow

  his 'cello a partner stepping out
    through the gap and clasping
      passers-by about their business.

Eyes Shut Tight
Elgar's Cello Concerto

So easy to list emotions
                      from melancholy to indignation

      in the end it's water –
rain to river to sea to sky again

      tears are breaking

you are there
           under the spotlight
                      lost and found
                                  in that concerto
     eyes shut tight
    you dive without support

   discover the wrecks
     the beckoning mermaids
      the sharp reefs

   only to rise
          evaporate
                  become clouds casting
                  shapes of mythical, nameless
                  creatures across the sunlit
                  screen-slopes of the mountains

   falling to the watershed
        beginning of the river
  no maps have marked

              my son
            you open your eyes
          as you did at birth
            that May dawn
         I walked with the birds.

Nightclub Fairies

Saturday clubland Cardiff after the match
                                              hiatus of cheer
    before the blood and vomit
                            cops and hospitals
                                                  CCTV reality shows

                queues sheepdogged by bouncers
                    girls like peacocks
                        boys like peahens

          standing on the pavement
              waiting for a bus
                  that doesn't exist
                              roads are closed
                                    horns don't blow –
. **We're shit... and we know we are!**

        police in formations
                        like an army of occupation

approached by a fairy on a Treasure Hunt
    long-legged
             black tights
                    two pink antennae
                              Got a business card?

          joins her band of fairies
              white-winged and heavy with mascara
                they tick off the list together

                                    gotta condom
                                    gotta pube
                                    gotta bottle-top
                                    got toilet-paper

                what spell will these make, I wonder ?

                will it change them back into women?

                will they regret it later?

Chipoil Avenue

They're looking for a name
   for the road which runs through

    call it **Chipoil Avenue**
     call it **Obesity Way**
      call it **Heartattack Row**

  dump your kids
    give them a couple of quid –
     they can eat the trees
      till there's no oxygen left

       in the rolls are insects
        so many species shaken and collected

        you're a veggie then eat
         the containers or cups

         the wind moans litter
         the rats are plump
         and even the air
          is dripping fat

      DRIVE-THRU
          a box will take your order
          you will eat from a box
          your kids will prize
          a box with eyes

they're looking for a name-
  so how about **Cholesterol High Street?**

         (we only need a drive-in graveyard
          so they could shuttle bodies
           like dead animals
            dropping with the trees.

Einstein at the Comp.

When Einstein came to the Comp.
    he was slumped behind the curtain
        like a loose puppet
            but
                who would work him?

he was the clone
        of a brain
            left for research

    his relativity
            worked a light-bulb
        on a pupil's head

    "Bad hair day's every day!" he said
    "Bob Marley!" yelled a heckler
    (but his locks weren't dread)

    he was a mere nobody
            when he came upon the theory
        (all mere nobodies duly listen)

the planets were bubbles blown
  by a Year 10 girl
    who almost swallowed her gum
                everyone wanted time to stop
                before the next lesson –
                everyone wanted to travel in space
                and stay young

    the universe was a huge black balloon

  and, without saying,
           some delinquent burst it –
      believing he was the chosen one.

Encircling

"Imagination is more important than knowledge.
Knowledge is limited. Imagination encircles the world." (1929)
         Einstein

    No equation for imagination –
            its light
            immeasurable

     a microscope
      upon the stars
       in a single grain
yet
   what shapes are fashioned there
    no-one can claim
     by deed or sign
         the two heads of the atom
          exchange expressions
           are twins
         whose skulls are melded

  the embrace of a bird
   whose energy rings the world
          space never to be walled
           with mind of God

  reaching out
     into discovery of doubt
        a bed of dust
          the destination

  but always, always
      the infinite layers

   onward
     upward
       within

A Bonfire in Brittany

The beginning and end
                    this bonfire
                              a Saint's day
                                          a turn in the weather
    she watches it rise
                mesmerized
                              eyes aglow

          its waves of fire
          its spitting sparks

        she shields her roasting face

in it she imagines
              a cave   a hut

          she dances to the crackle
              of hedge-cuttings and twigs
    in later light
          she's a giant shadow
            with stilted legs

and afterwards
        like everyone else
                she is smoke

    through layers of clothing
            as if her skin were ashen

  her hair the colour of hay
    smelling of a stubbled field
      after the harvesting

  when the bonfire settles
        to a hive of light

    she lies on the grass
        as stars press
              honeyed fingerprints

    on her windfall face.

Kreizenn Ar Son
Cavan, Brittany

The triskel uncurls itself from the sign

    shape-shifts into an ear
            a map through the woods

a clothes-line of white paper banners
            clapped by the wind

    air becomes our instrument
            a single plastic mouthpiece
    in the hollow of bark and bank
    and pipes sound high and low –
    comical birds in the leaves

    above the cascading stream
    are strings
        whose colours are keys
        to the water-flow

            we listen close to moss
            for the slow   seeping
            diminuendo

    learn to value every rain-drop
    which drums on tins
    suspended from branches

        at an amphitheatre of ferns
        we play
            a xylophone of stones
            a log marimba

    substance and vibration
    the journey of an echo

    this is the forest
    of discovery of sound
            and
            silence
            also

Fado Singer

    Mariza
             with the poise of a ballerina

        casting the net
                    of her long black dress
              from Lisboa to Africa

  taut white of her hair
              pulled by those rope-braids

she sails
      her ship of song

               the plucked guitar
               the single drum
                              from the streets of Lisbon
    voice   a wind
              caressing
              tousling
              disturbing
                          the hair of everyone

    she twirls
        a bark taken
              never anchored
                        refrains rise and dip

  she flies without wings
    her large brown eyes
      like two discs
        reflecting the sun

    Mariza
        her alleyway opera

              the streets become water
                down to the harbour.

Komitas

One million voices crying inside his head
one million brothers and sisters lying dead

almost forgotten, unacknowledged –
was it guilt of not joining them?

the concealed nation
the fugitive nation
the murdered nation

he stands now in Yerevan
the Conservatoire bears his name

from bricks/glass/frames
come the songs of resurrection

into the cave he was thrown
with fellow poets, musicians

the murdered nation rising again –
music pushing away the blocking stone

shaped, moulded by a baton –
a choir curing the madness
25 years of dripping bloodiness

one million voices harmonising inside his head,
one million brothers and sisters: a requiem of red.

The Tears of Pablo Neruda

thanks to Adam Feinstein

The tears of Pablo Neruda fell

    but they couldn't quell
    the smoke of the Moneda Palace
    rising in snakes of panic

    they couldn't wash clean
    the bloodied, broken hands
    of Victor Jara, shot singing

    they could never carry
    the cortege of Allende
    past those silent signs

the tears of Pablo Neruda
as he was blocked en route
to his death from cancer

    could not rally the ghosts
    of the many disappeared
    for one last protest

    could never irrigate the desert
    or quench the thirst of those
    he once gave floods of words

    could not halt the bullets
    from Pinochet's mouth,
    whips of the General's arms

but could
        become
                a huge eagle
                      in his old house
                      (ransacked, ravaged)

talons ready
        to attack
                to come back
                        as he promised

each drop of water
            a feather flexing –

            "Neruda?"
                  "Here!"

Legacies of Pinochet

Hooded
      a Guy
           waiting to be burnt alive

     in crucifixion position
                to be nailed
                      to the wall
two ends of the circuit attached –
  jerking and jolting
              a psychiatric patient
              brain-blanked
              by current

kept awake all night
  standing spread-eagled
    a mountain bird
          snared
                its wings clipped

  white noise screaming
            a baby so starving
              its voice a blade
            cutting the throat
             from inside

     bent to the dirt
           a parody of prayer –
          made to eat
          dead skin
             stripped by razor-wire

prostrate and bare
       blood and bruises
              from down-pressing truck tyres
a gun in the mouth
     the bullet's whine
          no song   no words

        these then
      your legacies, General –
       these your hell.

Every Palm a Map

They took them away
        the coal and iron
                we were black and grey

     our rivers contaminated –
     fish like tarred lungs

used, abused
    the old colliers
        staggered up hills
            sat and spat from benches
                  gob in clots

      our mountains emptied
      we walked on waste
      precarious, ever-shifting –
    a slurry of closures, redundancies

we struck, we fought
    lines of blue bruisers
        waving their pay-cheques
           to bloodshot our eyes

      every palm a map
      of the Valleys

    (once ships of Empire fuelled,
once steam powered engines of trade)

        but now
    they look back, look down
        upon us –
      inward-turning folk
    huddled around our loss
like witches round a cauldron,
    brewing strange spells
       of disruption

  for every sacrifice
               a miner released
                             from his cage
                                          half-blind
                                                        to find his way

               every palm a map –
          scrumpled up, thrown away.

Up the Silver Birch

Peacetime Yossarian
                he loved to climb
                              up the silver birch
(he'd planted with his own hands
and now the height of rooftops)
                he climbed back years
                    to conker drops
                    to shaking windfalls
                    to filching plums
        not naked like the Bombardier –
            his uniform the smooth bark
            camouflage for his silvering hair

no-one sought him there –
everybody too busy
peering for a hole, a trap –
or narrow-eyed ahead
on the road to the next...
                        Peacetime Yossarian
                              he even slept
                            his zen meditation
                        of feathered dreams
                          becoming one
                              with cloud

      the silver birch
              half-llama
                      half-elephant
       took his body
              on its back
                      in its trunk

            nobody ever looked up
              to the bird-man
                the child-man
                  the dead-alive man
        the fork of boughs
           became wool
        as his thoughts fell
           one-by-one
             to seed
             below.

Glyndŵr Road

No way through Glyndŵr Road –
blocked by the Drill Hall
scuffed by marks
of a deathwatch tattoo

where are the sons & daughters now?
                                     the curved arrows on cars
                                           tell they're living
                                 in unassuming terraces –
                                    of C for Cymraeg
                                    of a Celtic curve
                                 of a red dragon's tongue

but **EUROPE IS MY NATION**
rebels against the rebellion –
as if, 'Aber is my city'
when all says smalltown

will they leave and climb
                         the followers of the sign?
how soon will commoners become
                         the newfound noblemen?

Glyndŵr Road leads to itself –
but time will come
when they will turn
their backs on the Drill Hall
(pink as Empire)
and move away
beyond sea   beyond mountains
towards a high-walled skyline
and down
into the city they can never
call home.

Dog-hour

    Four in the afternoon
                        but I share the city centre
          with **Big Issue** sellers
      and other down-and-outs
          with hats
        wide open stomachs
          few coins shine
             like needle-points

                    their stooping dogs
                            hang heads
                     like pack animals
              whose backs
                have been permanently bent
          by their burdens

it is February
        it is dog-hour
                on the pavements
                      from the drains
                       (like the once brewery
                          tea-bag smell
                            pervaded the streets)
  nobody buys the pound-bag bananas –
    maybe it's the rumour
      of snow on a north wind
        or Millwall supporters
          coming to trash the 'Owain Glyndŵr'

        dog-hour and only
                    a nearly empty
                    bottle of plonk
                      is insulation
                        is sleep-bringer

        winter's blue uniform
           the one
      you cannot change –
         its badge of terror.

The Remains

They gave him a form & said -
      "Go ahead! This is all you need."

    (he had once been Someone
    like the town itself –
      night sun of chimney flames,
      cannons to blow holes
      for the natives' chains,
      railways to girdle
        Russia and America

    he had once been a physician
    for every machine, diagnosing
      the faults and applying the cure
      with his scalpel screwdriver)

if he failed to go there
 they'd stop his cheque
  they'd check his heart
   they'd declare him brain-dead
   they'd delete his statistics

        (that time they sent him
         to slaughter cattle and pigs
          his hands shook like fish
           just hooked and landed)

    so he went to the perfect oblong
    of trees where the White Tip
    once stood (its lime
    sloped around, useless)

    he was told to dig
     in a rough patch that remained
     where dandelion, daisy and clover
     were unsung as ever

　　　　he dug deep unknowing
　　　　　　whether it was coal again
　　　　　　　or some rare strain of metal
　　　　　　he was supposed to find

　　　　　with a heron's sight
　　　　　　he delved up broken bulbs,
　　　　　an item of underwear which resembled
　　　　　　a tattered catapult long buried,
　　　　　a child's tricycle miniature chariot
　　　　　　mud-clogged & rust-choked,
　　　　　bricks in crazy-paving fragments

all the industries of his town
　　he flung onto a skip
　　　taken to the landfill tip
　　　　with its poisonous smells
　　　　　and cancerous seeps

　　　　　　　　　　　　　to burn, burn
　　　　　　　　　　　　as he shook again

　　　　　his whole being, not just his hands
　　　　　　a cow with diseased brain

　　　　　he had been fed on the remains
　　　　　　of his own kin.

Flags of Neon

      Above the town
           across the moor
                    below afforestation
         walking with speed
         no destination

except
    away
        from the darkening day

        the winter night
        fast approaching

        the only sound
          of croaking crows –
        vultures of our clime

                I think of Gwyn Alf
              his *shadow-communes* –
           how far away they seem

the two flags of neon
  block out in light
    the base of the town
               gunsmoke clouds
                    gather from the west

I'm alone on the brim
  of a tip
      tracked in coal-waste –
     with the brooding ghosts
       of Dissenters and Chartists
      who will not answer my requests

            streetlights are holes
              in the arms of the hills

  two flags of neon
        everglow veins.

War Stories

"We are our own last resort" – Padraig Fiacc

1. AHOGHILL

The TV newsreader said
            "Ahoghill"

    silence dead
               lake-borne mist
       of early morning

    tyres bald as monks
      unable to grip
         slither-skating towards
        a drystone wall

the police-station window

              (window itself so unusual
            in this province of wires)
                     cracked ice
   wall with black marks –
     sockets for eyes

Gaelic consonants of the name
of a village of flag-holdings
   aloft like raised graveside guns

I knew for every bullet-hole
         a ricochet
             in days and nights
                   to follow
   sleeplessness
       our square window
            a target

(the shopkeeper raised himself
  at a midnight calling
    for desperate medicine
        a hole in his head
            spluttering and spitting blood
    Ahoghill –
      the gutterals
        of a gasping
           for last redemption.

2. WIDOW'S COTTAGE

Who was she?
                  that pale painting
                    of a woman in mourning
                    eyes ever-following
                        our to-ing and fro-ing?

            house in the Moravian settlement
            the Puritan squareness of it
            the slate-hatted hardness
            and strictly no colours
                  (not even the red-white-and-blue)

  above flat
        a couple creaked the floorboard
        borders between us
        the lightbulbs shook
          but this explosion
            of cries and moans
            made us jealous

     in our single sleeping-bag bed
still
   from the frame
        she squinted disapproval
                at our sometime unison
     Gaelic Catholic & heathen

while from opposite flat
              came the sound
              of a flute-man playing
              up and down his stamping
              tunes towards the claims
              of fertile conquered land

   the rhythms of marching music
                  of love-making
a loom producing linen
              a redness seeping in
     of bloodied fist
              of a woman's season.

3. ST. JAMES'S PARK

They all sat around
                for the *craic*
                          words sparking
        the fire coughing out
          gusts in coaly fits

      she in slimness
             like her Da –
                    hair almost to waist
                          a fine curtain to draw
                              whenever she wanted away

neighbours were Aunties
   next-door an actress
      famous for 'Some Mothers....'
   no airs   just another

                        she'd been sent to elocution
                        up the big house on the corner
                        tennis-court in the garden –
                        failed to roll down
                            her *skrake of dawn*

      St. James's
           up the Falls
                    from terraces of Crimea and Bombay
                    constant reminders of Empire
                    where the troops patrolled
                    night and day

        radio ready on the mantelpiece
           the TV on, but soundless
              the News only streets away
until
    they fell like soldiers
       in No-Man's-Land –
         their parapet table
                  at the stammering automatic
                  cutting off their talk –
                        huddled in a living-room bunker.

4. THE MESSAGES

Stepping out of an evening just
  to do the messages just
          some cigarettes and a *Pan*
                                  she trod on a Brit.
        (past the holy water font
          front-door always open
            to the world and its weight)

  the soldier started
                turning his gun to point –
      as she hand-horrored
        in instant recollection
           of the man whose exhaust backfired –
        shot dead for a sniper!

the crouching soldier blocked her path
  as though he owned it
  and she'd had to dodge round him
    in a comic dance as he lowered
      his weapon at this girl
        in flares and flowery blouse
          much like so many back home
            in Manchester, London, Leeds....

                  up the tree-lined street
                    towards the Falls
                      and longing for toffee-apples
                        or the crunch of honeycomb

  not the burning of faces
                blackened in conspiracy
                              with the night.

Dust Anybody?

On the wall of the train toilet
                in meticulous Tipex
     without a phone number
       for the purchase of

   and if
       you responded....

            why would you want
              somebody's sheddings of skin –
              their days gone missing?

            what would you do
              with that precious dust –
              recycle it into a face?

            where would you place
              the grey smears of surface –
              over a clock's face?

            how would you explain
              the fact of bought dust
              in all its uselessness?

            when would you spread it
              so as not to appear
              a purveyor of death?

            which items to choose –
              the altar of the piano
              or the font of the mirror?

     who shares their dust anyway –
       somebody who wants their body
         to be owned by everyone?

Green-car

He's got a Metro
  he never drives it –
    it's got weeds for wheels

    he's got tomatoes
      he's got strawberries –
        they grow inside the car

        he always waters
          he always watches
            his greenhouse car

            he's got a carrier
              it's a white carrier –
                the only bag he takes

                he fetches water-cress
                  for his sandwiches –
                    from the land out back

                    it is a *cwtch* he says
                      a *cwtch* of water-cress –
                        this is his breakfast

                        he leaves by fences
                          he jumps over fences –
                            never along the drive

                            he stares at his path
                              stares at his garden –
                                they are overgrown

                                he's got a Metro
                                  he wouldn't sell it –
                                    it's filling up with green

                                    his name is Eric
                                      he was a postman –
                                        he delivers leaves.

The Groper

He came from behind
  pinching between her legs –
    her short skirt fanning

      she mouthed him off
        you could lip-read "Fuckin perve!"
        (a man in the line laughed)

          he swaggered away nonchalant
            and flicking a ticket to grass –
              grinning below his shirt

                (you could mind-read those mag's
                  he'd concealed under sheets –
                    those girls in gagging heat)

despite his gait there was a tic
  on his lips, you could limb-read
    his legs desperate to escape

      she shamed and alarmed him out –
        willing his crabby hand to rot
          his knob to drop off, food for dogs

            you could gesture-read her shrug
            "The pigs? Wassa ewse?
            They'd call me a waster!"

              he homed hard, the groper,
                while she brushed off his finger-prints –
                  seeds still clinging to her.

The Holes

       Where are the holes
                                in my head?
I can't find them
            if I did
                  I'd fill them
                          with lists   dates   engagements

    they are blanknesses
              pages unwritten
                  and a no-ink pen
                      I scratch with, to be let in

     names shuffled in a pack
                         objects disappear into their dark

          I blame anyone
          who's near

(since I gave up that Master Key
  it's been happening
                 I watch myself closely
                            I am my own bodyguard

        which genes wield the drill?
                        how silent are its bits?

         contemplate the tincture of daffodils –
         how to distill it
         with winter approaching

      I could burn the page which gloats and glowers

          it will not make me warm.

Cycle of Malcontents

        the water-wheel
        the treadmill
        the spinning of a deadly yarn

a house where water lays siege
attacks the roof and walls
invades with battalions of droplets
seeps like dropped propaganda
messages of condensation
dripping down windows and doors

    the casualties, the wounded
        bronchial, asthmatic, arthritic
        germ warfare under cover
        of the damp as the lungs
        slump and the joints collapse
        the veins bulge out

in retreat, the defeated
troop for their papers
for the signature
the pills and vials
        alchemy to promise
          water will be blood
           once more

    you can't step down, step off –
    energy's not made just lost

the chemicals combine
    like bellicose neighbours –
        you hallucinate the dank rooms
      a house owned by the elements

            the rain clots
            the wind coughs
            the cloud's a bruise
            in a sky whose skull
            forever aches in thunder.

Clouds Collapse

    Clouds fall down
                      remain
                                    grey rat's fur

no breeze to carry litter
                    to scatter
                                poisonous seeds

             clouds too heavy
        settle on the Heads of the Valleys
                a migraine

          the throbbing particles
          of smog

     each breath nauseating

  huge hole of the landfill
                      packed with Christmas detritus

packaging burnt
        now fumes
                occupy like an empire
                            conquering the air

our cars
      insects
            whose shells
                are pierced
                      by the smirching stench

     clouds collapse in heaps
                  snared by smoke

        rats' teeth clench roads
        as we choke.

Women of Bryngaer

    We may not wield the spear
        against fear of bandits or fierce tribes
          who would capture our fort

we may not be allowed
                        to guard the rampart

      but
          the circle would never be complete
             without our fires   our cauldrons
           without our delicate powder
              rubbed from the grains

so many of us die giving birth —
  ashes thrown into streams
    taken by the river to the sea,
      the place we came from
        so the druids say
         and so we return

                we are the smoke
                    which keeps vermin away

              we are the herbs hanging
                for taste and cure

              we are the reeds
                intertwining each home

              we are the daub
                hardening with the years

              we are the skin and fur
                around our children in winter.

A Shrine

                    the doors close
                       the smoke rises —
                    but she remains

"you'd think there'd be some closure"
        is what they say —
living is all remembering

                        each object left —
                    brush, make-up, perfume
                        awaiting her return

    I make a shrine
       in the spare room

ornate and draped in gold
   her dress   jeans   blouses
      hang from curtain rails

            the only offering is myself

    I smooth her clothes
       willing them to be hair

    the lines of photos
       I flicker from stills
          into movies of times together

    I wash away the present
       from my hands before entering

    I close the golden curtains
       place her coats over me as blankets
       and sleep to touch her again.

Star-searching

      The town lights
                 have taken over
                              from the stars
refused to don
        their hard hats
                in deference

        they have out-shone
                  the night sky

            a black hole
            in the brow
              of the Great Bear

(if I were a Viking
    I'd claim
the peg has been pulled
  on constellations' curtain)

but a bright glow
            from streets   signs   houses
   has risen like a gas
            and melted the rings of Saturn

      even the Milky Way's millions
         of stars
             so distant
                  so mysterious
                      to the probing lens –
                become a neon drive-thru

the Lion run over
       by a juggernaut

                  the electric field
                    the Plough must follow
                      is the furrow of streetlights

the North Star has been harnessed
          and hoisted as a night-club sign

    I search
              the gaps between office blocks
                above the towering flats

wait
    to be blinded
             when day comes.

Passing

Walking south
                        turn around
                           at the wooden jetty –
                       sea-anglers hooded
                          other side of harbour
                               appear to be cameramen
                              reeling in the scene
                                   with hook and line

walking north
               not into a dream
                           shingle and sleeper-vans
                           the foam
                           on-rush of breakers
                               wings of water thrown

as I pass him
        a ghost still living
                  met solely in dreams
                            these 10 years separate
             now he's scowling down
               at broken flagstones

    father   and   son
        passing where once
            he'd pushed me in a pram
not a word   exchanged

      white plumes of spray
                  disappear underfoot

as I hurry back
        glancing round
                  in case he should catch me

        raise me up
        in his arms
          again.

Oisín's Last Poem

Is this the land of Tir na nÓg?

on the shoreline
         upon white strand
                  elatedly wave-hopping
  with Niamh racing
           down dunes of Derryane
         her magical white horse
         formed from waves

(I would be ageless
   lose myself here
     like the native Natterjack
       with perfect camouflage
                 and I would make her a poem
                 out of the rocky heights
                  of MacGillicuddy's Reeks,
                with lines of fuchsia
                    growing wild along roads

        (but I must always return
       to a world grown old,
     must fall to ground
      bones like broken shells
     to find –
              my friends have long returned
               to stone in unkempt fields
                among daggers of gorse
                 and thistles' swords

    I will leave her there
      as the sun breaks through
       the Atlantic west
        beyond the Skerrigs
         like two dinosaur-backs

    I will leave her
      with her cowslip hair –
        as the white horses of water
            sink into night's distance.

The Scallop
Aldeburgh beach

      Past fishy smells
                    which tickle and slap
         lobster-pots puzzly nets
each and every
            folly house
                    fantasia pink and outside spiral staircase
                  the adopted lighthouse
                        bungalow where the lifeboat lives
    past all this
        and more
              pebbles scrunch and crunch
              repeating   "**Once,once,once....**"

         on the rise of the beach
         I took it for a wreck,
          the rusted shell
            of an abandoned ship
closer
  and its words leak light –
  it is the fisherman's heart
                (lost
                    still calling)

from land it is so calm –
  from one angle a squall
    from another a storm

              the Scallop's no place
              to scatter ashes –
            they'd be blown inland

                it begs you to sit
                in its ear
                to hear
              the coastal choir –
             treble of seagulls
          bass-baritone of breakers
            wearing down   wearing down

      from the Scallop
      you drink sound.

Diving into the Dark
Rupert Brooke in Granchester

Out from the orchard
   from the Vicarage
     from the still clock
      he ventured
               snuffling, shuffling
                 through the night
               stumbling on windfalls

   leaves whispering
the ghostly weight
    of Byron
  whose pool beckoned
            he aped him
                     lame-legged
            over the long meadows
             startled cows snortled
     icy autumnal breath –
  full 'O' lowing

        (in awe & fear
          like child Wordsworth –
      so much better to **live**
       his studies now
     than to be stuffed
        by some taxidermist don
      in a museum of learning
     where grass could not
    be walked upon)

he made for the green river
  to shed his clothes
    in the honeyed light
   of an apple-moon
        the Granta caressing, numbing
       releasing then clutching
        with freezing fingers

     opening a pathway
               diving into the dark.

Insomniac Jazz

Thanks to the Thomasz Stanko Quartet

The Midnight Inspector stalks me
   his words of condemnation
      a wire of worries
         entangling, snagging
                         I used to hear the stream
                             one step
                                      over the fence

         at the cliff-edge
       where he has followed me –
         the saxophone's siren
       beckons plaintively –
         snare and cymbals
       my heart-beats urging
         to fall, fall away

clipboard and razor-pen
    he notes
        my every move
        my every expression

                          the trumpet's high notes
                            tell stories of dolphins –
                            the melancholy bass-line
                              is tide moon-moving

             I cannot question him –
             the Midnight Inspector
         with his monotonous synthesizer drone.

A Once Strange Face
thanks to E.S.T.

You can travel to

     the edge of a cave
     the rim of a forest
     the stile before moorland
     the last wet sand
     the downing river-bank
     the brink of friendship
     the notion of a kiss

and throw a stone
 into the darkness
  of tree tangle
   of animal sounds
    of waves' hiss
     of rocky blades
      of risky rides
       of falling out

       you can wait
        for its drop
       or for the echo –
       but it will never
       come back to you

if you should follow it –
 tears become calcite
  hands of ivy climbing
   feet lost in mud
    skin barnacled by cold
     legs taken like twigs

but at the end
    a once strange face
        pulled up from deep

a once strange mouth
     drunk with yearning thirst.

The Boy & The Grand
from a photo by Philip Jones Griffiths

    Up   down
                up   down
                            the boy trampolines
                            on the Grand

      (while his mates pull and tear
        as if it had horns)

                      concerto of cacophony
                         splintered sonata

  the keys uprooted like punched-out teeth
  the strings slack veins left to dangle
  the foot of the pedal disjointed
    the wood fractured exposing white

            he conducts
                      and they ignite

        his fiery feet
                their matchstick arms

even the space
      where sound would resonate
                    is not spared
    the air chased out
          across the stale stench
                  of the smouldering tip

he leaves the Grand –
        a carcass and a coffin
        both broken

                only the wind
                      the reeds playing.

A Manic Conductor

My heart
>   is racing
>   away
>   from
>   me

      I don't know where it's going –
      if I will catch it

  it's a timpani
      ignoring the score

    I wave my arms
    a manic conductor
    trying to get it back
    in time

its tempo
    makes me breathless

        when I'm still
        in rest
      it beats blind up the mountain
      I can't hope to climb

        its fierce solo
            a warning.

Gorse Grows Back

Though it is burnt so often
                gorse
                          will grow again

        on the slopes of Penparcau
        it was tunnels
        it was dens
                    the hedgehog spines
                    of its Spring emergence
                          pricking our bare legs
    we hid for cover
            snipers of the gun-tongue
            clicking lips
                      of live and dead

and now the smell
  of smoke spreads
    across valleys –
      gorse charred
     mice and insects, foxes
      all become ash

                in Antrim
                      each candle-petal
                      was lit
                      for a victim

              the bushes marked the coastline
              wild lights
              knowing no direction

              they starred our Sunday walks
                away from flagstones

  and now
        despite the fire-alarms
        the choking air
                    here it enlightens
            roadsides   roundabouts

        children burrowing like rabbits
           under its spiky threats

      children armed with matches
         destroying with scorched-earth curses

all those amber tips
              and green palms
                            those hands helping me back.

Acknowledgements

Acknowledgements are due to the editors of the following publications where some of these poems first appeared: *Poetry Wales, Planet, Dream Catcher, West, Red Poets, The Seventh Quarry, Merthyr Writing, Red Banner* and *Long Island Sounds* anthology 2009, *A Song for Owain: An Anthology of Poems for Owain Glyndwr* (Y Lolfa, 2004)

Also by Mike Jenkins

A Dissident Voice
Invisible Times
This House, My Ghetto
Red Landscapes: New and Selected Poems
Wanting to Belong (Fiction)